House and Home

House and Home

by

Sheri Flowers Anderson

BROADSIDE LOTUS PRESS
Detroit

Broadside Lotus Press

Publishers since 1965

Copyright 2023   Sheri Anderson Flowers

First Edition

Naomi Long Madgett Award Series Editor: Gloria A. House

Book Layout: Leisia Duskin

ISBN 978-0-94-713-30-7

BROADSIDE LOTUS PRESS

Post Office 02011

Detroit, Michigan 48202

www.BroadsideLotusPress.org

DEDICATION

For houses, homes,
and the families within.

CONTENTS

On Grandma's Porch

The chickens, out of their gated coop,
roam in the small, fenced yard
round and round the house, where we –
my grandmother, mother, father,
and great aunt – sit in green painted
metal armchairs on the front porch. The
talk is about the news, soap operas, heat,
the peas and tomatoes in the garden;
or they ask me about school or say nothing,
nothing at all, sit in the silence
of a late morning in a rural town
on the old porch
of an old house that belonged
to my late great-grandmother.

A Saturday morning in time,
where my grandmother's black,
misshapen bare feet are momentarily free
of her scuffed men's leather house shoes,
while unworn fluffy pink and fluffy yellow
house slippers lay wrapped
in dusty shoeboxes beneath her bed.
Her mason jar of ice water sweats rings
on the gray, painted concrete. The chickens
peck at the grass, curiously, studiously,
as if each time around the house, around
that small green yard is a new world.

Hands
(For my grandmother)

The black hands of the pianist
at our church amble
across the keys. Slender fingers,
clear polished nails, joy, rushing,
building, singing.

I am watching hands.

I have a black and white photo
of my grandmother when she was younger.
She is pretty, a dark shade,
her face resting on her hands.

Hands that I watched
knead dough, milk a cow,
wring a chicken's neck,
dig a shallow grave to bury a dead dog.
Hands that cut out pattern pieces for quilts
and sewed quick stitches.

She washed me up and plaited my hair
with hands that broke off switches and
didn't spare the rod.

When she turned 65, many years ago,
when I was in college and in love
four times a year,
when she had been widowed, twice;
when my hands had grown steadier
but not my life, when her life was steadier
but not her hands,
she began to take piano lessons.

On good days, when her hands didn't ache,
she practiced the same song
she sang in the mornings,
"What a Friend We Have in Jesus."
She never really got good at it,
but it made her smile.

I never tried to learn piano —
perhaps one day I will; but my hands,
less steady now, remind me of her hands
and I remember the gift.

The Lilac Bush

My great aunt Orza Lee was a bully.
My grandmother was not.
The two shared a small inherited house
off the country highway.

The lilac bush grew large
by the front steps of their house.
My grandmother loved it.
My great aunt did not

and one day began the job
of chopping it down.
She ordered my father to complete
the work and he did so, with his saw and sweat,
burying its remains in an uneven gravel grave.

I was 12, too young to speak up.
The wafting smell of lilac
while sitting on their front porch
was one of my early loves.
The bees loved it, too.

Years after on summer days
I mounted the steps of their porch
toward my great aunt's satisfied smile
and my grandmother's powdered hug,
longing for that purple scent.

My Aunt's House on Charles Street

She must cut them regularly
to put in vases on her tables, the roses
that now bloom all over her yard.
A recent venture for her,
a new investment of her time.
Each room I enter, I breathe deep
at the threshold, fingers touching
door jambs to steady myself.
The house is changed, a small remodel
after my uncle's passing. My uncle,
a testy, dark man, his pulsing radius
quieting my young cousins' laughter.
The hardwood floors refinished, my heels
clack where my aunt leads me—
We enlarged the back room here—
where a closet used to be somewhere
with a curtain as its door
that housed Monopoly, checkers,
and my cousins' cotton dresses.
We often played jacks near that closet,
near bunk beds once in this corner. Or there—
I'm dizzy from looking sideways,
missing memory out the corner
of my eye, disoriented between
history and change, larger rooms and
southern exposures, where rose-scented
spaces have renewed themselves.
The kitchen has a larger window
to the backyard, where a birdbath
blooms with a splashing bird, where bushes
bloom with roses. My aunt
opens wide the curtains to all her rooms
bathing them in sunlit renewal.

We All Pass Through, Unnoticed By Most
(For my grandmother)

The quilt she'd made
is faded from use,
softened with loss,
a reminder of her,
of how most of us fade
into graves of thin memory.

Before her death,
we thought we'd never forget
her look, her smell, her voice.
After death, threads once strong,
are now broken in segments,
yet hold invisible
her legacy of warmth.

The Thought of Charred Remains

Halfway to work she'd worry
that she left the iron on or the stove
or that some electrical mishap would create
a smoldering fire in her home that would rage
unnoticed by neighbors until it was all-consuming.

Everything was fine. But the thought of
the charred remains of photos of her youth,
or of the children growing, growing,
the ashes of refolded letters, frayed journals,
the gatherings in scattered shoe boxes
created a sinkhole in her heart.

And perhaps this was the day
she should turn around or
she should have grabbed
all her latest poetry,
every draft she had in progress,
as some kind of emergency backup.

Otherwise, she'd be haunted by memory
in cloud formations or smoke
or the vapor of words on windshields
that drift by when she's driving or dreaming,
that provide no hint, no sign at all, about the point
where she was too far removed
to save anything by going back.

Uncle

He usually drives by my father's house
on Saturday afternoons and honks—
honk honk—
as is done in the rural areas
like Wrightsville, Arkansas.

His car, a huge blue Chrysler sedan,
speeds down the two-lane
country highway, past my father's
small brick house, on days I'm not there
and days I am.

On the living room couch with my father,
he drank his last beer in front of us,
his small dark head tipped back.
He told his stories and joked, his unsteady frame
vibrating with his loud, husky,
sing-song laughter that could be heard
across streets and possibly
through closed windows.

He slapped my father on the shoulder
and their booming laughter
harmonized, their heads
tilted back, gasping for breath,
eyes watered with joy.
Then my uncle, scratching his
wiry, gray beard,
backed his car
out the gravel driveway.
Two quick honks goodbye.

He went into hiding, avoiding doctor's visits,
dyinga slow death of seclusion,
bottles of Jim Beam hidden in the car
that zooms down the two-lane highway
through sparsely populated rural towns.

He thinks we don't know
that he speeds up when
he nears my father's house.
Sometimes I catch the sadness in
my father's eyes.
Or on the road I catch a shadowed glimpse
of my uncle in his zooming car,
his braced black profile
staring straight ahead, his thin hand
on the steering wheel, waiting
until just past the house
to honk.

Hitting Nothing but Air

The father yells, gets into the rusty gray Thunderbird,
gesturing for both boys to get back.
One of the boys, who had been standing perfectly still,
darts inside the sagging house, head down.
The other boy, his mouth opens,
then his 9-year-old voice breaks through:
No, I want to go with you, Papa! Please!

The father pauses, then curses as he starts the car,
rolls up the window against the small dusty yard,
against the dirty boy. As the car lunges
into the street blasting dust and smoke behind,
the boy swings down, wildly snatches up rocks,
his bare feet not feeling the jagged yard
or rough street beneath him.
With all his might, he throws rock
after rock. One hits the hollow metal bumper.
He throws another, then another, moans,
hitting nothing but air.

Baby World

He picks up every little thing
and puts it in his mouth!
She says this again of her youngest
as she shakes her head,
not smiling. We watch
his 10-month-old form
an amusing case study:
he's low to the ground,
sometimes crawling,
sometimes scooting,
a microcosm of
curiosity, a compact
wanderer, a discoverer
of lint, gum wrappers,
torn shoelaces,
missing battery
covers, his eyes wide
open, scanning, forming
a world in front, a sculptural
question of found items,
eye-catching white
things and round things
and silver things
and fuzzy things

at auntie's house,
the auntie who hasn't taken
time to pick up after his two
older brothers' playing,
smiling at the science
presented by clutter,
the experimental taste tests,
swirling each found item
over his lips and tongue
just as we grab it from him—
us with the protocol,
he without concern for
housekeeping or danger
or dirt or manners,
all risk and adventure
on to the next discovery.

Vanity

I touched my lips
to a cold window,
caused a lightning bolt,
started a storm.
The violent reaction
between hot and cold—
though it might have been
coincidence.

List Poem for Stay-At-Home Orders
*(Remembering the Great Toilet Paper Shortage
due to COVID-19, Spring 2020)*

So definitely
extra toilet paper.
And sanitizer.
And liquid soap.
Face masks. Lysol.
Prayers for everyone.
Yoga pants.
The T-shirt
with the grape juice stains.
(Or spaghetti stains?)
Text messages.
Phone calls. Emails.
Curbside pickup.
Canned goods and snacks.
Word-find puzzle books.
Netflix. You Tube.
Naps. And more snacks.
Less gas mileage.
Walks through the neighborhood.
Waving to anyone who'll wave
during walks in the neighborhood.
Zoom meetings or classes.
Oh – and Amazon.com says hi.

For the Authors of Books I Love

It's not that I'm in love with you
except I am. You don't know me
from Eve, but your words
fill me, stretch me, a stifled moan
let go on its own accord,
a rainbow mist before me
a breath heard and seen.

I've been looking for you,
listener and architect of words.
I'm breathless when reading you,
my hair windswept,
my mouth open, my body prostrate
before your worded altar,
before your linguistic cathedral,
but I gather myself before anyone sees me,
breathe normal—inhale, exhale—
then turn your page.

Poly-Silk Red Flower

The roped pots hanging
from their hooks on the pergola
remained emptied of hope
after the unnamed plants died.

Eventually, to fake the lushness
that never returned,
I bought artificial greenery
and fake red flowers to put into
the shallow graves of the pots.

This new presentation through
the kitchen window
was more colorful and acceptable.
But in my cleverness,
I didn't count on the hummingbird
dipping its beak into my betrayal, into
that poly-silk red flower again and again.

I didn't count on nature's intelligence
confronting my artificial reality,
exposing my pretty and petty deception.
Yet after a few moments,
the bird flew away – away –
as if there was nothing to forgive.

The Junk Drawer

In the kitchen junk drawer
is a plastic tray with an assortment
of loose screws and mysterious
metal fasteners that have somehow
worked their way out
of their original housings,
of their careers that held something
together.

They fill the tray like a collection
of found treasures
with the premise (or the promise)
that one day we will find
where they fit, find their place
in the world, put the lost with the found,
tighten a loose mystery.

These sacred pledges we continue to make,
continue to pack into this drawer to hold,
imagining that someday we will fix everything,
every *thing,*
while we remain oblivious that something
somewhere is falling apart.

A Fixer's Gift
(For my father)

It didn't matter what broke.
He had a tool for that.
A tool to fix the car's brakes,
replace the tire, test the battery,

a tool to replace the cracked
windowpane in the living room,
or some loose doorknob
or a bathroom faucet.

On the odd chance
he had no tool, he would
jimmy-rig it, a fixer's gift,
a prayer in loose parts,
a practical need for wholeness.

Even for crying eyes or runny noses
he'd have a clean handkerchief,
which he'd quietly offer,
his calloused hand
momentarily on your shoulder.

Looking at My Father

When I look at him through the eyes
of a middle-aged daughter,
the him retired in his blue recliner
in a well-deserved, well-practiced nap,
while the familiar rerun of Perry Mason
he sat down to watch drones on without him,
I see the laugh lines carved
in his mahogany cheeks, a hollow remnant
of his loud, booming laughter.

I see the worry lines on his forehead,
a shadowed tattoo, symbolizing the real deal:
the weary life of supporting his blackness
and his family, a son, a daughter,
house and home, dealing with my mother,
an unhappy wife, through the silent liquid
of Crown Royal or Budweiser after work.

Now, after years of abstaining from alcohol,
He breathes steadily between the armrests
of church work and the kinder obligation
of volunteering. This inhale of freedom,
a statue of liberty.

The life-lines etched in my father's face
provide hints of his story,
the quiet conquest of life's mountain climb
to his comfortable chair, where sleep
holds echoes of war, always war,
or the booming laughter of his youth,
and maybe a private space for all those times
he was not allowed to cry.

He Will Not Talk of His Childhood

To know that my father was once a little boy
surprises me still, though I stare at the proof
in black and white. This photograph,
maybe from 1948, is the one picture
that we know of, the one picture
of him as a young child at age seven
or eight, maybe nine, with the same nose,
lips pressed together, big brown eyes.

I'm old enough to know that this is so,
but it surprises me still, that he had first days
of school, that he learned his alphabet and math,
that he practiced and practiced the cursive handwriting
that I love to see him write. That he did chores.
That he was probably shy and scared of the dark.

In this photograph he's not smiling, appears lonely.
A lonely black boy, born out of wedlock
to a mother too young, to a father
not acknowledging him while living around the corner.

He was a good boy, I'm sure. Yet he will not talk
of his childhood when asked, claims he can't recall it.
I'm certain he was well-mannered, but too soon a man.
And that this photograph that I love so much,
that he will barely glance at, is, for him, nothing
but a phantom memory.

But in the Evening

The front room
with its window
facing north
never had enough light.

A morning walk
around the block
in bright Texas sun
helps curb
the cloudy feeling
inside, as does

the best seat
in the house,
in the kitchen
by the bay window.

But in the evening
when dusk settles,
the house absorbs
the night,
devours 100-watt
incandescent
halogens, fluorescent.

We leave lights on
in every room,
then complain about
wasting electricity,

in unconscious efforts,
distracting ourselves
from unnamed sorrow.

We Don't Talk

We eat, snack all day,
the art of the chew in our ears.
From crinkling potato chip bags
we swallow salty words,
the fear of speaking our heartbreak.

We stay busy in the back room
or the front room, separately,
eyes on phone, ears for separate plans,
while TVs drone to cover
our stubborn silence and
the fear of speaking our heartbreak.

We vacuum the beige carpet,
lift the dust of our lives,
the humming fear of speaking our heartbreak,
the dredges of our unsaid words lifted
into the full canister, our collective collateral.

This whirling noise of cleanup and order,
is our deepest conversation.
Instead of speaking our true anything,
one of us — it all depends —
answers with a louder volume on their TV.

Stubborn Pride

Anger is reheated in the microwave
on Corelle dinner plates,
then chewed with the rice and chicken.

We dab unresolved issues
into paper napkins, torn
tissue hints at the corners
of our mouths.

Resentment is swallowed
with iced tea, our glasses neither
spotless nor blameless.

At the round table, a sound table
without corners of retreat,
we do not stay long enough
with heads bowed.

We do not say enough
over our communal leavings of crumbs,
where apologies and forgiveness might be
offered over the polished grain of wood.

Instead, we excuse ourselves,
chairs scrape the tile floor,
and we wipe the table clear
of our presence and reconciliation.

Bushes in the Backyard

The bushes in the backyard—we don't know
their plant names—have overgrown the fence again.

Signifying the weariness of our lives,
rambling, mounting too high with neglect.

Once more, we rented the chainsaw
to tame the overgrowth that for several seasons
and unspoken reasons we ignored.

With the heavy motorized tool in your gloved hands
you were unbalanced on the grass, the step ladder,
as you severed the waxy, green-leafed limbs,
with the whirring, sawing, gnawing of late action.

I dragged the cut branches around front for the truck,
our sweaty forearms scratched and scarred
with the clawing consequence
of another avoidable stretch of inattention.

Weary and Far Gone

Free of a three-day fever, of my bed,
my husband's soup, my heated rooms,
the optimistic escape outdoors found me weary

and far gone, further than my usual walk
around the neighborhood,
a circle larger than life.

The houses were familiar and strange, quiet
and closed. One man in his driveway,
wearing a knit cap and thick sweatpants,
worked under the hood of an old red Mustang.

He never looked up. Not even when his
tail-wagging dog sniffed my knee,
offered quiet acknowledgment.

That unknown curb did not welcome my rest.
I couldn't lie there on the cold slab of sidewalk
where only a stranger's dog had taken notice of me.

Its heated fur gone, my bed far away,
I stepped slowly, steadily, like a meditation,
one footfall after another toward home.

Legacy

If my father
wrote poetry,
the lines on
his forehead
might disappear,
and he would finally
know
that something like paper
could hear him.

If my mother
wrote poetry,
her anger
might tear the pages,
bleed through
to the table
as she wants us
to bleed, her words
carved deep
into the surface
until a semblance of
that deep love follows.

When I write poetry,
their combined legacy,
that shadow of pain
seeps through my ink.

Breath of Sorrow

After midnight last night
on the old Pine Bluff Highway,
where there are no streetlights
nor many houses,
I drove over a dead animal
too soon before me.

Usually, the shadows
in headlights are nothing
when I reach them.
But that momentary shock
absorbed under the wheels
was a thing, a something,
in stretched darkness,
a life and death that
I drove over and drove from,
leaving the scene,
like the driver before me.

Unable to see in the rearview,
I drove on with the breath of sorrow,
black tire marks
on the night road
in memoriam.

Ghost

Grandpa and I were in the shed
when a gusty mid-morning spring wind
slammed the brown metal door shut,
forcing the rock doorstop outside.

In the echo of the jolted aluminum walls,
Grandpa James said, "It's him."
The him that Grandpa James often told about—
a Johnnie Ray who, after
his young wife killed herself
and their baby, or—
my cousin's version—
after the white men caught up with him
in a drunken fight, in the middle
of some long-ago night,

somehow reached the top steel rafters
of the small bridge that crossed the stream
and hung himself—or was hung—
using someone's tie on the uppermost crossbar.
The ragged evidence of the ghost story—
a frayed strip of fabric—twirled
from the bridge's rafters for all to see.
Hold your neck, my cousin would say
when we drove across the bridge.

Grandpa murmured, half hummed,
as he fiddled with the mower,
while I looked around, held one of his tools.
A shovel that leaned against the shed's wall
slid, fell over, clanged against
the concrete floor,
and a cloud of dust floated.

Chatway Nursing Home

Hazy, watery eyes stared
at the window.
I was afraid to meet

the unattached sorrow.
She glanced,
retreated, eyes slow-

motion back to the window.
I poured water, hand damp
over hers, cupped around
the red plastic.

She took a trembling sip, didn't
know me, wondered if I was her
daughter or granddaughter
or nurse.

Through the window
across the field,
a playground pulsated
with squeals and laughter.

Through the window
I watched a small boy
leap from a swing,
legs forward,
up, up in the air like Superman.

Toast to the Unhealed Past

When he and his three graying brothers
from out of town get together,
invariably they tell the same stories.

They turn meat on the grill,
drink beer at the patio table and
one of them laughingly starts:
Do you remember the time?

It could be any one of them that speaks
of what is now called child abuse,
how their mother, my mother-in-law,
in her fury at some unclaimed infraction
would line them up when they were young,
(when one got in trouble, they all got it)

and she'd whip them, all four boys in a row,
with an extension cord or a belt,
then send them to bed without dinner, and
explain and complain to their alcoholic father.

To this day, they are connected still
by this bruising history and aching hunger,
their mother now disconnected
in a cloud of Alzheimer's
and a fleeting memory of good little boys.

With the dignity that remains, they laugh,
raise their beer bottles in a toast to the unhealed past.
They high-five one another over the table,
over the hysterical humiliation
of their happy home.

One Day You Will Tire

Every time we see you,
you are running away,
high heels clacking across driveways,
dragging your three young sons
behind you, with their shoes untied,

young black boys,
trying to stabilize themselves
on elementary school playgrounds
and in classrooms, looking for answers
everywhere they go, in the cracks
of the sidewalks,
or the pages of their school workbooks
while you hide in the smoke of your
drug use and financial insecurity and in the
broken promises of their absent fathers.

We talk, but only sometimes now—
not like we did before—
with our unwelcome advice, with homemade bread
or thirty dollars for gas.
Your face constantly turned away
in defiance and in the despair
of an artist who doesn't make art,
or a mother who can't make a home.

No matter how fast you run, you can't
separate yourself here
from yourself there. You stack
corners of various new rooms
with your duct-taped boxes of pain.
You carry your rage and fear in the soles
of your feet, your underground burnished
with the rushed steps of restlessness and eviction.

Sometimes, but not like before,
we repeat our exhaustive prayers,
imagine that one day you will tire
of this marathon of escape, turn around, allow love
and your recovered self to overtake you.

This Boy-Man-Child

The long stretch of road
before the turn to get on the highway
extends for maybe two miles
through the quarry's chalky fog.
Several mornings on the drive to work,
around this curved road with
no homes or buildings nearby,
I've seen this boy, this boy-man-child,
walking on the sidewalk, his dreadlocks
skimming his collar, his cheeks and ears
vulnerable to the cold, frosted air. He might
be 21 years old. In my rearview
he could be 15. He wears quarry
gray and tan, a pullover sweater
or light jacket, a backpack on his back.
Where is he going?
Where did he come from?
If I were bolder
and slightly crazier, I'd stop my Toyota,
hazard lights flashing on the road,
and run to him to zip his jacket,
press my warm hands against his cheeks.
But would I scare him to death,
interfere with his destination?

Grandson Number Two

After you've helped
with his vocabulary words,
then fed him leftover spaghetti
and homemade bread,
he stares steady, through you,
through charcoal eyes,
seeks more knowledge
more connection, more.

He's eager to hug,
easy to hug, warm inside arms,
as if he gleans information
inside that cocooned embrace,
as if he listens for
secret code in adult heartbeats.
You feel him growing too fast,
time-lapsed, beneath your chin,
stretching, pressing
against the limiting curve
of your sheltering arms.

I Come This Way All the Time

The setting sun grays out the highway,
but today the grayness, the pressured speed
of passing trucks, shakes me and my small car.
I come this way all the time,
but in the shaded light of dusk,
the highway and its exits seem unfamiliar.

The yellow and white wildflowers
that freckle the springtime expressway,
that sway in a gentle breeze
in the valley of median grass,
blur past, unnoticed at 70 miles per hour.
This is no time to stop and smell them.
This is a highway, for crying out loud.

Don't ask. I don't know why I'm crying.
I feel as if I've missed my exit, but
perhaps today I should miss my exit.
Perhaps today I should drive far away,
past all known exits, where this highway
turns into another, where I'm wind
and witness to wildflowers.

That Kiss

The way you kissed me—I remember it well—
the way I was stunned into silence,
and how, before that kiss, I thought
you'd like me better if I wore higher heels
and shorter skirts. I thought you were like that,
preferring the superficiality of a magazine centerfold.

Except the kiss -- that kiss ushered me
into an entirely different world,
lifting me to my bare toes,
the carpet's static electricity beneath me.

Now, I stand before a mirror, stare
at the lines in my face and cherish you,
you long gone, barely a shadow
of your reflection left behind.
I still feel you, your arms snug and insistent.
How we held on for dear life!

Lost

Such a brief encounter
this strange dachshund in my yard,
fat, obviously cared for,
graying around the snout,
whiskers like a grandfather,
but no collar, no tag,
no home for the moment.

We looked into each other's eyes
for several seconds. Confused, I
brought a bowl of water from the kitchen.
This stout wiener dog drank
at this front door rest station,
staunch on those impossibly short legs.

I hoped he would stay on our doorstep
(maybe the owner would find us),
but the dog left, journeyed on
beyond our street, beyond
where we could find him,
far and quick on those unbelievable legs.
Eventually, I emptied his water bowl,
but for hours I kept looking out front,
lost and abandoned.

What Sits in the Corner

The wheelchair
in the corner of our garage
is streaming with cobwebs
and dusty neglect.

The disused black spokes
of the still wheels in the corner
taunt me and my wife-hood.

He, with mild cerebral palsy,
ignores the threat
of what sits in the corner
as he walks from his car
through the garage,

leaning into the lightweight
cane he favors, leaning
into his natural inclination
for normalcy, for mobility.

Yet he stumbles
over dangers
that I can't save him from,
legs that won't cooperate,
tumbling across unsound ground.

Leaving me separate,
sorrowful, a witness to a crash,
to determination, and to pride,
to what goes before a fall.

Rhythm of Gratitude

It's the best place,
the pillowed dark,
this downy space

when his soft snore begins
on his side of the bed
and I smile—
the familiar blanket
of his breathing warms me,

this simple rhythm
of gratitude.

No one asks why I smile
in the dark.
It's just because.

The Heart of the Matter

Months and months
of an oppressive, undiagnosed illness,
a lethargic un-wellness, a long
loss of appetite and many losses besides,

when a night of heart palpitations,
out of rhythm with my husband's snores,
had me awake at three in the morning.
Once again I was afraid
I'd be dead before daylight.

So, of course, I got up
to get my last glass of water, sipped it,
standing barefoot on the vinyl kitchen floor.
I stared at the ivy plants in the bay window.
They were dying—had been dying.

So, of course, I found scissors
to clip, commiserate with dead leaves,
and pale stem cuttings, which I put
in jars of water, lining them
along the window over the sink.
The cuttings limped with indifference
to my dark, predawn dilemma.

Later, hours later, I woke up, still breathing.
Not dead. Not. Dead.
My spouse was preparing breakfast.
And the clippings—the clippings. Perhaps,
it was only my imagination,
but it was necessary that I saw
tiny, tiny hairline roots sprouting
in their water jars,
as if my life depended on that hope of nature,
on that morning kiss, that scissored start,
that tilting pale toward the sun.

On Being a Widow

I mean I miss
the momentary back rubs,
the warmth of your hand
on the spinal pain between
my shoulder blades,

but maybe I sleep better
now that you're not here. Or maybe not.

The void is wide open, expansive enough
for both wakefulness and dreams

in the absence of your maleness
not pressed into me at two in the morning,

in the weightlessness of your forearm
no longer resting across my side,

in the empty air where your fingers
no longer seek my belly and breast,

in me not fetus curled
while you embrace me in sleep,

not folded inside your
singular reach of us, not matching
your rhythmic breath.

My solitary breath—I hardly hear it—
continues without you,
the way memory of that slow dance in our dreams
lingers within my skin.

What I Meant

The pillow-top cushion of the mattress
is fluffed with overdue notices, good intentions,
what I meant, what I meant to mention—

I meant to have a cup of chamomile tea,
the taste of it in my mouth. So I promised
tomorrow there would be tea,

steaming, honey-sweet tea, in my sun-colored mug.
I make other promises while I'm at it,
promises in the fatigue-kissed warm sheets,

the digital clock pushing time red and blurry.
I hope to remember the insistent press of your lips,
pay the insurance, be kinder and less hurried

and more generous; to buy groceries for the food bank,
to write more poetry and to not kill the plants again;

to sleep well through the night, wake up
rested and clear, like a cloudless blue morning,
to start again—again—with new grace.

Weight

My purse gets heavy
throughout the week
carrying too much
that might be needed:

a temporary carrier
for loose change,
receipts, tissues, lists,
leftovers of indecision
the weekly weight of worry.

Hurry makes for a heavy purse—
misplaced reminders,
the gravel of grief, the trash
of people's opinions,
the endless personal packing.

It fills to near capacity,
a strain on the shoulder,
past the point of reason.
Then—eventually—
it's emptied, cleaned, put in order,
to prepare once again
for what might be needed.

New Religion

One recycling bin at a time
is the way I quietly decided
to save the earth—
seeking the small triangle imprint
with the numbers from
one through seven,
as some religious symbol.

It was a calling,
this compulsion
to reduce,
re-use,
recycle,
this effort of repentance
for the costly tragedy of landfills.

Yet it's questionable,
as religion can often be,
the way I place small offerings of
appropriate, rinsed recyclables
at the altar of blue bins.

It's questionable, this constant search
through the enormity
of our daily disposal and profit
and our insatiable convenience,
for the unaccounted sorting of
what can be saved, reborn.

Place

Every two years or so we moved.
As a military family we were ordered to arrive
at a new place, a new base, where the number
of other black military families varied.

Each move multiplied my virus of fear,
the infinite zero of shyness. At each new school,
it took weeks for my trembling lips to speak.

My father has long retired, but new places,
new spaces reinvent my anxiety,
create an irreversible exhaustion, a binding tremor.

Avoiding travel has been a disservice—
to my son, whose mind is closed
with the comfort and familiarity of the same streets,
the old neighborhoods, friends
from elementary school, remembered
crushes on blonde, blue-eyed teachers—

and to a lonesome me, my fear an island,
my timidity shored
by the illusion of being safe,
surrounded by my own self-centered history.

Nomad
(For Louise)

Her purse is a small leather backpack,
a symbol of her feet of flight
She moves constantly, imagining the next
everything.

She's unsettled after days and months
in one space, tugs at the cage
of a signed lease.

Her sparked energy, like a struck match,
is the gypsy in her who seeks to new.

She pushes forward, whether it's
store to store or street to street or
city to city, her car's gear shift
in go mode—go, go, go,

while I stay put. She's restless,
her wanderlust in constant search
of a homestead, but not a home;

in search of the various walls
of temporary shelter, the embrace,
of repeated first loves and infatuation
with new spaces.

I seek an old love, a history of home.
Different levels of comfort.
Maybe neither of us is truly free.

Rain

A thousand miles from the raging
wildfires shown on the six o'clock
news, thunderous rain
pummels our new flowers,
the flowers that pushed
through the dirt near
the brick-lined driveway
to bloom in the sun
that was too hot this time of year.

A rain
that beats away dirt
and bends stems,
flushes dust into streaming renewal,
smashing pink and yellow and green
into their muddy soil of origin.

A rain
that overruns roads around the city,
flooding gray impassable
intersections, high water crossings,
stalled cars.

We are all seeking middle ground.

Everyday There Are Mourners

Sirens and flashing lights
of police patrol cars barred
the unimportant errand
for good reason, barred
the shortest distance
between two points—
the traffic light and Walmart.

A pickup truck's front end
was smashed against
the telephone pole.
A white car, crushed
and twisted, faced
oncoming traffic.
A bumper—
somebody's bumper—
lay in the turning lane.

Later, the evening news story:
"Fatal car accident
on Thousand Oaks.
Many mourn the death
of a substance abuse counselor
who was killed
when a drunk driver
ran a red light."

Wreaths are now nailed
to that telephone pole,
funeral flowers staked
to make a point on that grassy curb.
Everyday someone is missed,
someone failed to arrive.
Everyday there are mourners
at the corners of all our streets.

A Life Unfolding

A life unfolding
in recalculated journeys,
mapped in red and blue veins of
meandering meters, moving,
always moving.

This daily awakening and walking.
Uphill. Many heart-beaten paths
between feet and brain,
between butterflies and stars,
between coffee and hard conversations.

For better. For worse.
Veering toward misstep and grace,
toward falling, toward failing
again and again, toward a free-fall
of disorientation and loss and then,
the startling wreckage of surrender.

Why I Love Elephants

It's the National Geographic documentaries,
the filmed stories of the adult elephants
guarding and guiding the baby elephant,
the calf, the largess of parental protection.

It's the way they stick together, a loyal
herd of sisterhood, brotherhood,
elephant-hood, priesthood, quietly connected,
by elephant-speak and memory,
lumbering across the land.

It's the way elephants roam.
Or should roam. Freely. Truthfully.
Royally.

It's the way they stop me at the local zoo,
halted by their universe of gray
leathery wrinkles, where I stare and stare
breathlessly, through the heat-waved stench
of their steaming massive dung—a pile of it—
it happens—in the fake safari prison.

It happens.
Even in our human dilemmas.
In any dysfunction,
the elephant in the room
majestically awaits acknowledgement.

Night Terrors

He screams, walking the hall
at 3 a.m., the nightmare hour
for three-year-olds
with night terrors,
as the doctor called them.
Even when I grab his hand and
walk him back
to his room, where two nightlights
and his teddy bear await,
even when I cradle his small chin
in the crook of my finger
and tell him it's okay,
he doesn't see me
and remains in the middle
of sleep and terror and tears
until I lift him and he softly
moans into my pajamaed shoulder
until sleep comes.

A 2 a.m. Memory

It was easy to slip out of bed,
feel my way down the hall
to my teenager's bedroom,
to step gingerly over shoes,
clothes, schoolbooks,
and hit the radio's off button
to silence the screaming DJ.
As a mother, I'm the author
of sweet dreams and poems. Yet
it was not so easy,
after this particular guardianship,
this hike in night's wilderness,
to get back to my own dreams.

I stood there
in the middle of the hallway,
in the middle of the night,
in the middle of the almost quiet
of the creaks of the house,
in the almost quiet
of the wind outside,
in the almost quiet
of the family's soft snores,
where it was not so easy
to return to the dream of the poem
that possibly woke me.
So this is what I wrote instead.

Parenting a Teenager

Without an argument
we were not speaking.
A dark gray between us.
I checked windows,
for cloud cover, for rain,
surprised by the framed
sunlight and clear blue.

He conserved words
with me. I was concerned
with lack of language,
our misfired connection,
our mistrial of communion.
So silently I prayed for him,
angry prayers, to connect to some space
around him or over him or by him,
to nourish my intimacy with words
to quench my thirst for speech.

He would walk by me,
his stride unforgiving,
giving rise to my smoldering anger, my need
and greed for acknowledgement
and talk, tipping near the edge
of tears. He would close the door
of the bedroom he slept in,
as if it were that simple
to keep the fire of my raging prayers
from getting through.

After His Mental Breakdown

When he returned from the hospital
after his mental breakdown,

the house was hushed.

The prescribed pill bottles on the counter,
appointment cards on the fridge.

Our worries spread onto the kitchen table,
covered with snacks, receipts, unopened mail.

Our unsaid words steeped in hot tea,
and hot baths.

He, medicated and fearful,
slept most days, most of the day,

head under sheets, curtains drawn,
to avoid facing his face, this place.

It was too much, he said. Everything

was too much. To hold a conversation
or eye contact. To explain. Who could explain?

As his mother, I felt the shushed aftershock
in my throat, tremors in my chest.

I burst into tears in front of the mirror,
navigating the complicated task
of brushing my teeth.

My tired eyes revealed what I hadn't known before:

That my prayers for his recovery were for *me*,

that a loved one's mental breakdown
may be your own.

Where Black Lives Should Have Mattered

Once in our family board game of Sorry,
we substituted a dry pinto bean
for the missing piece in the game
because something had to be done
to fill the void and carry on.

We are not sorry to be black in America,
but we're nervous in our own country.
Over and over, we're sent back to the beginning
of seething hatred, where the legacy of lynching
is worn as a badge by many.

In this so-called land of the free
and home of the brave, we are surrounded
by domestic terrorism and expected to smile,
to somehow believe that God made a mistake
about us. Yet there is no mistake,
except the intolerance and the voice of hatred.
For this, America should be sorry.

We fill graves, these black holes,
with black bodies;
fill them with fear for our black children,
and our unending grief and rage.
Black holes for black lives taken,
where humanitarian justice and dignity
for an American citizen should have been,
where Black lives should have mattered.

We fill these holes with what we can gather
so that we can carry on. It might not sit well,
it might not look pretty, but it's what we do.
We pour into this void our buckets of pain,
our broken heart fragments, and also
our multiplied, multicolored voices.

I'm Waiting

Come get me—
you with the open mind,
the kind heart.

Yes, you. The kind one,
the brave one, the one willing
to have the hard conversation,
willing to walk together
in hopeful understanding
in this racial and social unrest.

Come get me.
I'm sitting on the curb
waiting for you, for some relief
from this toxic whirlpool of intolerance.

You, with your truth-telling self
and me, with my weary, angular anxiety
as I smile at the faces of loathing,
try not to be killed in its violent stronghold.

Meet me for coffee, let me say hello
to the milky aroma
of warm authenticity, to the land
of the free, home of the brave.

Meet me somewhere
at the corner of happy and healthy
or at least at the intersection
of facing reality and being real,

so we can practice—and practice—
acceptance, connection, knowing,
that higher ground of care and prayer.

Come. Get me. I'm waiting.

A Little of Us

A little of the day remains in night,
some sun in the moon.

Even when dancing is over,
we hum the song or we tap
our foot when no music plays.

And in our children. A little of us.
The mischievous grin, the foods
they love or hate, perhaps the walk.

Our long-sought wisdom, our rehearsed
lectures, which we hope will remain with them,
usually won't.

But a little of us, maybe a dimple
on the left side.

Later

Later, when I think about this poem,
I'll be embarrassed.
Not yet comfortable
in the right to speak,
the right to express,
even though words
spill from my skin like sweat,
leak from my body, leaving puddles
of poetry everywhere.

I have more vision when I hold
pen and paper than I do
when I get new glasses;
yet fear and shame are prisons,
or prisms? Where light can
still get through?

I want to know, I want to be known,
but I don't want to be noticed.
I mean I can fake it, but later,
when embarrassment shrouds me like a sweater,
I'll withdraw, shrink back into a false humility,
cower into a dishonored black skin,
a subservient womanhood,
a shy girlhood, all violent lies for
a disappearing act, for reversing presence,
erasing space and place.

A different choice is
to fight the good fight of faith,
so that maybe later
when I think about this poem
it will be a step, a small step
toward home, toward being ok
in the skin I'm in.

Before Departure

What happens to a woman who thinks
she's going to die soon? Unfamiliar
with this script, she might situate her life,
her bank accounts, her regrets. She might
welcome the authentic, become more true
to herself (wear her hair in its natural state).
She'll probably kiss her grandchildren more,
licking sticky lips of abundant love.

One thing is certain: She'll search
for things. Old photos. Dingy letters.
Lists she made in her twenties.
Her soul must be hovering somewhere
in a dark closet impatiently, having waited
until this late day to be claimed.
A story must be pieced together before
departure. She has to mean something.

She might enjoy her food. Pray differently.
Pay closer attention to cloud formations.
She might scrap many of her to-do lists—death
is a great excuse for not doing a lot of crap.
Over a cup of tea, she'll apologize to her
found self, her new soulfulness, and for the lateness
of the hour. She'll swallow steamy regret
with each honeyed sip, but feel grateful still,
for she, unlike many, had a chance
to find her true self.

Full Speed Ahead
(For Claudia)

She reminds me of a train—
not the kind that ambles
along the track
at slow miles per hour,
but the one that barrels
full speed ahead, with the bright
beautiful, smiling headlight
of destination,

the whistling horn bellowing
its joyful presence—
coming through, coming through—
at the intersections of highly
populated places along the journey,
and at the crossroads of empty,
lonely, rolling spaces.

I admire her face-forward
trek, the rhythm of her wheels.
Sometimes, when I'm in my car
waiting for a train to pass,
for lights to stop flashing, I can hear her
laughter at her latest adventure,
and in the train's metal cadence,
I hear love, love, love, love.

Ashes to Ashes

In all practicality
being cremated when I die
is the obvious choice—
a funeral without
the ceremonial burial, without
the elaborate age-worn
mark of a head stone.

An intangible mark
is preferred. A life lived
as a single raindrop
that may have helped
water the growth of another.
A whisper of peace and prayer.
A spark of laughter
and kindness in the air.

Then gone.
But a final goodbye
marks a new journey,
requires the flash and majesty
of fire, smoke and ash.

Grace

My mother tends her vegetable garden
in men's tennis shoes and a baseball cap
my father no longer wears.
Her aged beauty sunned and warmed
among the green rows, she inspects leaves
and stems, steadies support posts, pulls weeds,
swats insects, spritzes vinegar and water.
She hums or sings a hymn, her eyes
constantly roving for snakes and a quick exit.

She suspects a rabbit watches her work,
waiting for its own meal from this garden.
Every year she mentions what my grandmother
often told her: that when you plant, you plant for all—
insects, birds, animals, bold kids.
Every year, the same story. Every year,
the same enthusiasm, digging the earth,
pouring in care, anticipating the transitory grace.

And Now We're Beautiful
(For my mother)

Some of us waited for years
for that butterfly flutter
in the cocoon-wrapped
skin of disappointment,
waiting to burst
with the belief
that we could fly. Or dance.

We are stronger than we think.
Now that our skin is no longer
smooth but mapped with
experience and now that
our muscles are limber but sagging
from the weight of our lives,
beauty is found
to be singular. Specific.
Personal to our heartbreak.

With aged bones,
there will be dancing,
dancing that will renew the marrow red,
that will carry the water
of our unending grief.
Our skin will sweat with
the balm of goofy laughter.
Our hearts will enlarge
within the wingspan of well-used arms,
surrendering outside expectations
of beauty, because it was always,
always an inside job.

Home

"Home, in one form or another, is the great object of life."
Josiah Gilbert Holland

The mess I make is devoid of order but is not devoid of me.
It's my domain. And I can explain. I have too many dreams.
Ideas flutter by. I follow. I lose time when I straighten
and clean, scrub and organize, so I drop clothes where
I strip, shoes where I step, bags where I stand, mail
where I've stopped. Surely there is some order,
but I cannot relay it to my home yet.

There is this thought: I don't care. Not hostile nor bitter,
but warm and unburdened and maybe a little defensive.
I'm exhausted and really, sometimes I just… can't.
My mother's suggestion: Pick up a thing or two
on your way to another room. It's on your way, she says.
Good theory, as my mother bubbles over with good theories;
poor practice, as I am not insulted by things that need
moving or adjusting or revising—I love creative process.

However, I am insulted by some things that no longer require
a place in my home and instead require a clearer disposition.
I pile them for Goodwill, trash dumpsters, divorce court
and promptly deal them out, over my clutter.
Acquaintances are surprised at my social decorum,
what I keep, what I toss, never neatly prepared for company,
let alone House Beautifulized.

Some say the state of a person's house
is the state of a person's mind. Yes. There is a lesson here.
I'm frazzled. Disoriented in my own skin. Afraid
of letting go. I want too much but have to make a living.
I cannot find the scissors or the tape, the mate to a shoe,
the teacake recipe. But still I write random poems,
find some comedy to laugh at, read books in the bathroom,
review art books in the kitchen, read Bibles in bed,
design clothes on my lunch hours, make collages at midnight.

I honor the thick path of papers, books, fabrics, art supplies,
between the living room and the floor beside my bed
that marks my way, my ambivalence in having a clean,
orderly house or having all things I love and think of,
admire and dream of, about me, present, presents,
presence of mind, to process and gather at random
fringe moments to remind me I'm here, longing,
searching and creating and gathering. I gather,
I gather until my arms, my home, my heart overflows.

Previously Published Poems

"Vanity," published as "Flattery," in *Voices International Magazine*, 1983.

"A Little of Us," published as "From Everything," in the anthology, *Voices Along the River*, 2005.

"Before Departure," published as "True," in the anthology, *The Dream Catcher*, 2006.

"We All Pass Through, Unnoticed by Most," in the anthology, *Inkwell Echoes*, 2019-2020.

"On Being a Widow," published in *Six Fold Magazine*, Summer, 2022.

About the Author

Sheri Flowers Anderson earned a Bachelor's Degree in business management, with a minor in creative writing, at the University of Arkansas-Little Rock. For many years, she developed her writing skills while working full time as a human resources specialist. She has won numerous awards for memoir and short story writing as well as for poetry. Her poems have been published widely over the last several decades, including in *Voices International Magazine,* and in *Voices Along the River, The Dream Catcher* and *Inkwell Echoes* anthologies. She is retired and living in San Antonio, TX.

9 780940 713307